Davor Antunovic

Hypnosis

A German Approach of Easy and Safe Usage of Hypnosis for Selfdiscovery!

1. Edition

1st edition
Author: Davor Antunovic
Translation: Martina Müller
Proofreading: Dragan "John" Cizmarevic, Manuela Schwarz-Brassat, Antje Lepschy
Layout: Mayir Aras
Fabrication and Publishing: Books on Demand GmbH, Norderstedt
Printed in Germany

ISBN: 9783842381414

Dedicated to my loving mother, lying in coma since December 2009.

Used Symbols

Explanation of used symbols.

 attention

 timing

 explanation

 technique

Foreword by Jack Elias,

It's always a pleasure to read a new hypnosis book that clearly will be helpful to a wide audience. It is even more gratifying when it clearly advances a deeper understanding of human potential. And when the presentation is simple and straight-forward, it becomes even delightful!

I believe it was Einstein who said something like "Find the simplest solution, but not too simple."

In Hypnosis: A German Approach of Easy and Safe Usage of Hypnosis for Selfdiscovery!, Davor Antunovic succeeds at presenting explanations of hypnosis and simple yet powerful scripts for its implementation. He makes hypnosis simple, but not too simple. He includes all the essential points that will make the reader comfortable with the possibilities of hypnosis and confident in their attempts begin to master the art and skill of hypnosis. Nothing important is left out.

I first became aware of Davor's work through online correspondence. I was impressed by his diligent and extensive reading in the field of hypnosis over the course of many years of study. And I was very gratified by his generous comments about the part my book, Finding True Magic, played in his growing understanding of hypnosis and its application to maturing spiritual growth.

The techniques of hypnosis are wondrously simple. All that is really needed is our willingness to befriend ourselves and "turn inside." Entering into a hypnotic state has the potential of taking us to the wish-fulfilling core of our own being---the creative power that can make virtually anything possible in our life.

To make this kind of contact, one's intention becomes all important. In my study of meditation and hypnosis over a period of 45 years, I have found time and again how a limited intention narrows the possibility of obtaining great results. Having a limited intention is like going for water to the ocean with a tea cup, not realizing the ocean will give you its entire self.

Limited intentions are based in limited world views and limited views of what we are. If we hold to a view of being small, frightened, lacking, and unworthy when we enter the hypnotic realm, we may not recognize the presence of this truly sacred inner power and we may not create a very expansive or deep request.

We need to have a vision of greater possibilities pointed out to us - possibilities of great accomplishment and possibilities of recognizing the greatness of our true identity. Davor clearly understands this and includes scripts to guide the reader to crucial aspects of inner potential: the Inner Warrior, the Higher Self, and the Quiet Voice Within.

If you practice with these scripts you can revolutionize your life beyond your wildest dreams. And since this can be challenging and even fearful at times, Davor, in his wisdom, includes scripts to help you cultivate an inner security of The Safe Spot and the protection of The Protective Shield.

Surprisingly few books point us in the direction of our spiritual potential and identity. In this world, material gain and sensual enjoyment is much more alluring. Of course, there is nothing wrong with material gain or sensual enjoyment in themselves. But our pursuit of them often includes an aspect of running away from our fears about our own short-comings and our belief in being small and flawed. So in an ironic and tragic way, succeeding at material gain and sensual enjoyment can reinforce our negative beliefs about ourselves. Davor makes connecting with our greatness a central point of his book and for that we all can be grateful. His choice of scripts opens the door to the possibility of deep healing and deep self-appreciation that dissolves fear.

Take your time and live with the inner journeys Davor has composed for us. Gently set aside any desire to go fast, to get somewhere or to some great experience. Our greatness is already accomplished, the challenge is regain faith in ourselves so we can simply relax and open to it and feel its constant presence. Even the most natural organic response to relax fully can be challenging for humans. Have you ever envied a cat's ability to relax? Often, relaxing thoroughly and deeply is all it takes to recognize the Presence that is always surrounding us and to feel our own goodness, and Davor has included instructions that will enable you to master the capacity to relax fully, like a cat!

So, I say again, take your time with each of the exercises and journey's that Davor has offered us in this wonderful book. Be generous with yourself and patiently welcome the richness of your own being that these guiding instructions are designed to bring into your feeling awareness.

Contents

Contents

1 A Journey's Beginning

Welcome to this experimental little book on hypnosis. A while ago a patient asked me if it takes special abilities to perform a hypnosis, or if anyone could do this.

"Yes", I replied. My patient looked back at me, puzzled, and asked what I meant by that. I replied "Yes, it takes special abilities, and yes, anyone can hypnotize another human being!"

In fact, it doesn't take a lot of previous knowledge to change into another state of consciousness.[1] We do this all the time:

- when we tell a bedtime story

- when we tell others about our vacation experiences

- when we tell spine-chiller stories at a camp fire

- when teaching a certain knowledge, that we present especially well

- and so on

There are countless examples of steering people into another state of consciousness. This can happen knowingly as well as unknowingly.

Every single one of us has at least once managed to bore someone else in a conversation just as well as fascinate someone and captivate with a topic. Basically, all these examples are changed states of consciousness. Here, hypnosis is not a special case, but follows a certain course, a ritual and a certain mood, that is beneficial for hypnosis.

---

[1] A way of experience that is determined by perception, self-awareness, alertness, capacity to act and intention.

2 What Actually is Hypnosis?

The following features can be found with every hypnosis:

- There is a certain ritual character:
- There is a pattern: induction–deepening–technique–ending
- Hypnosis animates one's imagination and leads the hypnotized person to execute certain exercises with the help of his/her inner pictures
- Most of the time the hypnotized person feels relaxed, but of course all kinds of emotional states and vegetative concomitants[1] are possible.[2]

And that is it: That's the whole secret about hypnosis!

---

1 This means all physical reactions, such as sweating, crying, trembling, changed respiration, laughing, etc
2 The techniques described here are positively intended to produce a good feeling in the hypnotized person. Techniques with possibly negative concomitants should only be used in professional, therapeutic guidance!

3 What Happens During Hypnosis and is it Dangerous?

A lot of half knowledge is spread about hypnosis and this is what makes a lot of people anxious about it. The best known German newspaper, for instance, has published many articles on hypnosis—but scarcely a single one of them has depicted hypnosis in a good way. This is in spite of the fact that a newspaper does exactly what hypnosis does: steers people's state of consciousness towards a certain topic and a certain emotional state. Unfortunately bad news sell better than good news. This is not necessarily because of a craving for sensation and bad news, as often claimed, but because of our survival instinct. Our consciousness and that of our ancestors was trained to pay more attention to negative information than positive information, because negative information implies danger.

In most cases, hypnosis is depicted as negative by people, who profit from other people living in guilt, fear or bondage—and guilt is a strong motivator.

Half knowledge about hypnosis causes most of the anxiety

Maybe you want to take some time to think about these words before you continue reading. In my opinion, hypnosis is a medium for brain users, not only brain owners. This medium belongs to an enlightened age to provide people with all the possible ways to develop in a positive manner.

In human history, hypnosis is one of the oldest means to healing. Hypnotic techniques are believed to have been used since the Stone Age. Hypnosis was used "scientifically" for the first time by Franz Anton Mesmer, a medical doctor from Vienna[1], Austria. 236 years later, in 2006, the German Advisory Board for Psychotherapy (Wissenschaftlicher Beirat Psychotherapie Deutschland) approved hypnosis as a acknowledged psychotherapeutic method. In Britain it was recognized 1957 and in the United States in 1952!

In human history, hypnosis is probably the oldest way of healing!

During hypnosis attention changes and is directed to a specific topic. The body and the mind are extremely relaxed. Today it is possible to measure the changes to brain states with the help of modern techniques.[2]

---

1 Around 1770
2 With the help of electroencephalograms (EEGs) and computer tomography (CT)

For the purposes of our hypnosis experiments, the alpha wave band frequencies of the human brain activity are of importance. This covers the range of 8 to 13 Hz[3]. This range of alpha bands is usually to be found when someone is slightly relaxed or in a relaxed state of mind, awake but with closed eyes. States of relaxation below this Hz level are referred to by theta waves (4–8 Hz). They occur during drowsiness and light sleep phases.

Using this book for hypnosis is about as risky as autogenic training or progressive muscle relaxation. It results in a very relaxed state of consciousness, that can help you to better access your unconsciousness. The hypnosis techniques contained in this book are about as dangerous as bedtime stories. In case the hypnotized person feels uncomfortable I would recommend taking one of the following measures:

1. take a walk

2. take a nap for 20 minutes (or even longer, but 20 minutes are fine)

3. eat something

4. talk to somebody

5. take a hot shower

6. take a hot and cold shower

7. take a hot bath

8. work

9. have sex

10. watch a good film

11. sun and fresh air

12. something else that makes you feel good

Hypnotic treatments like the ones offered in this book are guaranteed to be good for your health. Should you still have concerns, feel free to send me an e-mail to kontakt@hypnoenergetics.de or ask a physician or therapist in charge.

---

3   The normal frequency of an awake adult ranges from 13 to 30 Hz.

4 Let's get started!

4.1 The Structure of Hypnosis

As already mentioned, there are several steps to hypnosis. To make it easy for you, this book contains easy texts to ensure the four steps are manageable in a safe and confident manner.

The four steps are:

1. Induction

2. Deepener

3. Technique

4. Ending

To make things easier, the inductions are already linked to the deepener. The only thing you have to do, is to link a hypnotic induction with techniques and ending. So for these experiments you don't need to understand the complicated mechanisms of introducing a state of trance or anything complex. You can simply concentrate on the event, the experience, and observe how your partner (or participant or patient) reacts.

The following chapters contain enough information in each paragraph, that you just have to read out. However, to ensure the best result possible, you have to pay attention to several things when you read the texts.

Here are some useful tips on how to make hypnotic experiences as interesting as possible for your partner.

A good atmosphere is important!

- Allow your voice to be sympathetic. A good voice is very important and will make your partner feel comfortable and relaxed.

- Good background music helps to keep the room quiet. I recommend classical music or Indian sounds, as you prefer.

- It is advisable to shade the room, but with enough light so that you can still read the text. You could also use a sleeping mask, if the hypnotized person feels comfortable with it.

- Make sure that you and your partner are not disturbed. Turn off the telephone and plan your time, so that you won't be disturbed in the next 45 minutes.

- Essential oils can help to create a relaxing environment. Incense sticks are an alternative, but that is a matter of taste. Also, keep in mind that incense can cause some people to have headaches.

- The lessons are also suitable for use before going to bed. In this case, you can leave out the ending part and simply lead the hypnotized person into sleep. More information on how to do this can be found in the chapter called "ending".

- Some texts contain "Interactions", which are marked with speech marks: "Like this". Simply observe how your partner reacts and continue. In case your partner does not react as expected, ask him or her what is wrong or unpleasant and continue with the text once the problem is solved.

5 Inductions

5.1 First, simple steps

Allow yourself to close your eyes and to take a deep breath. It is exciting and important to simply feel relaxed and observe what is happening.

Tip: Try to match your partner's breathing!

Trust me, it is not that important to consciously listen to every single word. Your unconsciousness will pick out everything it needs to reach the perfect state of deep, hypnotic relaxation.

All right, together we will now experience hypnosis and I already know how surprised you will be, because it is so easy to reach hypnosis ...

What will happen now, is absolutely natural and normal and I ask you to use your normal and innate abilities to ensure that you go safely into a wonderful state of relaxation. When you follow my simple directions, you will slide into hypnosis. Of course you can resist this, but this is not what we are here for, right? Await reaction. If nothing happens after a minute, simply continue. *Now, allow yourself to be as comfortable as possible ... just keep your eyes closed ... for the moment ... and allow yourself again to take a deep breath ... before you can realize ... how relaxing it can be ... to just have one's eyes closed.*

It really is not important to quickly go into a hypnotic state. Your unconsciousness just knows ... takes its own time ... while your consciousness simply relaxes and listens to me ... or rests ... at a nice place ... which feels good ... from your memories or imagination ... a place of security and well being ... relaxing and good ... your own place ... an oasis of calmness in your mind.

Allow yourself ... in your own way and manner ... to arrive there ... a moment of calmness ... where I let you relax ... to arrive ... to find peace ... to gather your energy ... for all the exciting and relaxing things that will follow after that ... 60 seconds break *Allow yourself to relax even a bit more ... just realize in your own way ... how good it feels ... when certain muscles are allowed to relax ... while others take a few more moments ... are allowed to take a few more moments ... because this, too, belongs to a good relaxation ... not to take a relaxation too seriously ... to want ... to simply be ... in this moment ...*

... While your hands may keep to sweet idleness ... while they might still be moving ... in memories ...

While your legs are simply protected ... by socks ... and shoes ... simply lying there ... and maybe still have their own movements ... when they remember a movement ...

While the ears ... simply ... listen more closely ... when the eyes are closed ... and have their own interpretation of reality ... come back to memories ... from the past ... or your imagination ... while they still can sense all noises next to that ... surrounding us ... the background music maybe ... or noises from outside ... that, from time to time, find their way to us ... and assure us ... that life outside is still happening ... although it is not important now ... and in the same way, that you have two physical eyes with which you sense the world as you do ... it is easy to imagine we have something like an inner eye ... and this inner eye can see thoughts and ideas of your self, even when you are relaxed like you are now ... deeply ... relaxed ... and calm ... I like the idea ... that this inner eye, just like our real eyes ... owns something ... like an eyelid ... and that this inner eye is also able ... to close this eyelid ...

And when I now count from 1 to 5, you will slowly close your inner eye ... and it will become heavier the further I count down ...

Touch the space between your partner's eyebrows

1. *You can ... now ... begin to feel your inner eye ... just here, between your eyes, where I just touched you ...*

2. *When you close your inner eye, you will realize, that your inner horizon ... whatever it may look like ... clears and that this makes room ... for good changes ...*

3. *your inner eye now closes ... the more you relax ...*

4. *Relax ...*

5. *You now close it and be in perfect harmony ... with your most inner self and all thoughts and pictures blur and the new emptiness is a perfect basis for our coming work ...*

5.2 Hypnotic Muscle Relaxation

Imagine the big toe of your right foot and allow yourself to become aware of your incredible, innate abilities that allow you to completely relax step by step.

... simply let this relaxation slide further, into your complete foot, up the shins, allow yourself, your foot, your leg to become heavy ... heavy ... just heavy and relaxed ... feel completely relaxed and place weight of your foot on the area where it is resting.

It is advisable to give your partner some time, so read the inductions slowly ... as if you wanted to put him or her to sleep with it

Allow yourself, allow this relaxation ... this wonderful wave of relaxation, which began to arise a few seconds ago in the big toe of your right foot ... to glide upwards ... further up and up ... up unto your backside ... briefly tense the muscles in your backside if you want to ... just one second ... just like that ... and ease the tension and feel how your backside relaxes more and more ... let the wave of relaxation go on ... on and on ... more and more ... into the other leg and feel how your entire lower part of the body is completely relaxed and heavy ... heavy and relaxed ... very well!

... Let this relaxation go even further, allow the relaxation to move further ... up to your navel ... to your stomach ... relaxing further and further ... up to the celiac plexus, that is also called solar plexus ... but that is not important right now ... feel the weight of your solar plexus and of your stomach ... the weight and how relaxed your stomach can be ... how you can relax your stomach even further with every breath you take ... more and more ... further and further ... just relaxing ... because it feels so easy ... even side noise can be used to relax even more ...

Allow the relaxation to simply go up a bit further ... up to your chest ... slowly relax your chest ... breath deeply ... hold the breath a bit ... and gently breath out freely ... simply exhale ... and relax ... deeply and firmly relax ... feel your chest relaxing while you breath out ... simply relax ... With the next breath you take, let the relaxation flow into your arms ... Feel how your arms relax ... enjoy the weight of your arms ... feel their warmth ... relax your arms further and further ... your arms are becoming heavier ... and heavier ... heavier and even heavier ... now also allow your hands ... to become infinitely heavy ... just infinitely heavy ... and relaxed ... heavy ... and relaxed ... a good, relaxed ... nice feeling of relaxation ...

Now, that your hands and your body are completely relaxed, you can look forward to ... an wholly gentle and pleasant, welcome way of being hypnotized ...

just like ... you need it right now ... in your own way ... simply experience ... this nice ... and comfortable way of relaxation further upwards

... relax the muscles in your neck ... your right ... you have the skills for it ... simply relax the muscles in your neck deeply and firmly ... relax deeply and firmly ... every single muscle in your neck ... just relax ... simply let the relaxation spread further ... to the back of your head ... which is becoming heavy now ... up to your face ... now also relax every muscle in your face ... entirely ... relaxed ... in peace ... simply enjoy ... this deep, hypnotic sleep ... very well ...

5.3 Remembering a previous Hypnosis

You can use this induction, if your partner has already been hypnotized. *Maybe you can remember your last hypnosis very well, but in any case, it is easier to go back to this memory when you close your eyes. Would you like to do this now and simply relax for a moment?*

(Await your partner closing his or her eyes)

Well done, thank you.

Now, allow yourself ... maybe only partially ... to imagine your relaxation under your last hypnosis ... maybe you can remember how it felt, when your arms became heavier and heavier?

... or how your idle hands ... pursued their own interests ... whatever that means to you ...

... and I am not sure, if you have already discovered, how your breathing has changed in the meantime ...

... when you come to you ... and I give you one or two minutes ... to relax ...

(one minute break)

... and while you lay here ... and relax ... and use this hypnosis to the fullest ... because it makes sense ... to use this time ... it is good to know ... that every time ... that one uses hypnosis ... you gain additional skills to be easier and better hypnotized ... and while doing this ... it is really not important ... to do so as quickly as possible ... because this is not a contest ... hurry ... is one thing ... and hypnosis is ... another one ... and hypnosis is just a way ... to give hurry ... however hurry looks like ... the chance ... to get slower ... while you simply relax further and further in the meantime ... and discover your inner universe and your brilliance ...

... and I will now begin to count down ... and when I do this ... you will feel, how you get relaxed more and more, just like last time ...

    5 *You can now begin to again feel the weight of your inner eye ... comfortable and relaxed ... calm and in complete harmony ...*

    4 *When you close your inner eye, you will now realize, that your inner horizon clears and that this makes room for positive changes ...*

    3 *Your inner eye clears, the more your close it ...*

2 *And ... you close it even further and further ...*

1 *You now close it and you are in perfect harmony with your inner-most self and all thoughts and images blur and you now ... create a perfect basis for our work ...*

6 Techniques of Hypnosis

Techniques of hypnosis are meant to be read after an induction. All techniques are meant for self-experience and to increase self-consciousness and self-worth. They do not replace a psycho-therapeutic treatment, but can of course support it. Every technique definitely is worth a trance experience. You can either ask your partner what kind of experience he or she wants to have, or choose one yourself.

Further explanation of the techniques:

- The safe spot: The basic script to feel safe and comfortable in one's unconsciousness. In case of need, you can bring your partner back to this safe spot at all times with the simple suggestion "Okay, now please go back to your safe spot. You are going to feel completely safe there!"

- The inner warrior: At some times in life, it is important to face challenges. The inner warrior is our inner source for courage and energy.

- The higher self: Every single one of us has the inner need to have something more in oneself than what we are able to show. The higher self connects us with our best qualities and properties.

- The quiet voice within: When the world is the loudest, we often forget to listen to what feels right. This quiet voice within reminds us of what feels right.

- Hypnosis to improve learning: Who doesn't want to learn better and be more relaxed? This text gives us a new consciousness for what really matters.

- The protective shield: Sometimes it is hard to distinguish oneself from the surroundings and the doubts caused by others. The protective shield script can be of enormous help.

- The inner observer: An experimental script for discovering a so called "superposition" of the observer.

- Self-confidence: A high level of self-confidence is very valuable. This text will help your partner to develop and strengthen his or her desired level of self-confidence.

- The temple of healing: The ability to stimulate one's self-healing powers is anchored in our universal consciousness since the beginnings of mankind.

6.1 The Safe Spot

This is the basic text, which I put to practical use in a slightly modified way. The text creates a form of security and contentment for the partner's contact with his or her inner world.

Now ... that you slowly drift away ... more and more ... allow yourself ... for yourself ... to just let your thoughts flow ... all by themselves ... because they can do this so well ...

... ever since your birth ... some people come ... and some people go ... others are there all the time ... others are there just for a little while ... stay in your consciousness ... and are forgotten again ... some are gone in just a split second ... just ... because they can ... and we ... try to simply put them in order ... keep ourselves busy with it ... for a while ... who knows for how long ...

It is strongly recommended to use this text for the first hypnosis!

... maybe some are asking themselves now ... how deeply one can go into hypnosis ... and if this is already far enough ... this experience ... to really be hypnotized ... while it is important to know ... that the unconsciousness has its own way ... of absorbing information ... and that you don't need ... all this close listening ... because your unconsciousness looks for all the information it needs all by itself ... in the right moment ...

... always ...

... and now can even optimize this experience ... and by this I invite your consciousness ... to simply invite me to this exciting discovery ... into the depths of your unconsciousness ... when the inner horizon clears ... and you can arrive ... at a place, that we will call your safe spot of energy from now on ... a spot, where you can feel safe and comfortable ... sheltered and relaxed ... a nice place, that might also only exist in your fantasy ... or in reality ... that is completely up to you ...

... It is all up to you ... the complete energy ... a place, which from now on can serve you as a source for energy and as shelter ... that you can imagine every time ... when you decide to visit it ... even without my help ... a place just for your best ... with all the possibilities to find you inner security ... and now I am going to be quiet for a while and you are able to get to know your place a little better ...

Here you can wait a little and then ask, if it is all right to now continue or stop the trance. Alternatively, you can let your partner describe his or her safe spot, maybe you want to discover it together?

6.2 The Inner Warrior

The inner warrior is the archetype of a protector and of male energy. Once awakened, he helps the experiencer to distinguish him- or herself and to fight for goals worth living.

... While you relax ... further ... and further ... your body ... your mind ... gliding into this relaxing ... good ... state of relaxation ... you can simply go to your personal spot of energy ... your own place ... of complete security ... of perfect peace ...

You have come here to get to know a new part of yourself. A part that has always been there, but that you might have neglected so far.

I speak of your inner warrior!

Simply allow yourself ... to relax more and more ... look for a place ... in your spot of energy ... a place, where you will meet your own inner warrior ... a place that was made for it ... chosen by you.

Observe this place for a moment ... shape it just like you want it to be ...

In a few seconds your inner warrior will appear ... just imagine that a blue pillar of light appears in front of you and that a blue, luminous gate forms in front of you.

A figure is stepping out of this gate ... this is your inner warrior ... What does he look like?
Let your partner describe the inner warrior.
What do you feel, when you see this warrior?
Let your partner describe his or her feelings.
How does he move?
Await the answer.
Now, become the inner warrior and observe yourself. What do you think as the inner warrior of yourself?
Await the answer.
What would you like to say to your self?
Await the Answer
What else would you like to tell your self?
Answer
Now, change back to yourself. Did the inner warrior somehow change?
Answer
What would you like to ask your inner warrior?

Answer

What is his answer?

Answer

Would you like to ask him anything else?

Possibility for further questions

What positive properties does the warrior have?

Answer

Which of these properties are you going to need in the near future for positive changes?

Answer

It is time to say good-bye to your inner warrior. But before he goes to the place ... from where he will work for you ... from now on a bit more consciously ... he gives an object ... a weapon ... a weapon, that from now on will be a symbol for your progress ... what weapon has he give you?

Await answer

Observe the weapon for a moment, what does it look like?

Answer

What properties does this weapon give you?

Answer

Now, become the weapon ... What message do you have for your owner?

Answer

Change back to yourself now and look at the weapon again. Did it change somehow?

Answer

Good, now put the weapon away and say good-bye to your inner warrior for now. Thank him, that he, from now on ... also a bit more consciously ... will be with you ...

6.3 The Higher Self

The higher self is a superordinate program, which helps us to look for the best in ourselves, which surprisingly enough is already within us and does not need to be looked for outside. This text will give your partner deeper insights into his or her existence.

And while you enjoy this deeply relaxing state ... allow the sound of my voice ... to guide you into this state ... that will let you be completely perceptive ... to be conscious about the presence of your real, inner I ... to help you and your body into ... perfection of ... this relaxed consciousness ...

... starting now ... simply ... pay attention to ... the sound of my voice ... and every tension in you will loosen up ... while you might still note one or two outside noises ... and if you simply look at what you are doing right now ... you will realize, that you only do all this for you, for what is best for you ...

... and your higher self is always present ... no matter if you are aware of it ... or not ... to give you what you need with the help of instructions and support ... to help you to free yourself from the sorrows and problems of everyday life ... these unnecessary restrictions ... that are ready to be removed ... to ensure that you can retain that, which guides you on your true path ...

... letting loose ... dissolving ... whatever it takes ... to get rid of the problems right now ... feel your body breathing, if you want to go even deeper into relaxation ... let your unconsciousness re-evaluate your sorrows and problems for this healing ... be aware ... by the light of love ... of your higher self ... by this ... or another way ...

Begin with a feeling ... begin to be aware ... and imagine ... how your body is surrounded ... by a white light of purest life energy ... and exactly this life energy ... is getting more and more visible for you due to different ways ... and when you feel better with every breath you take ... when you imagine this light around you ...

... you can be surprised ... but surely, you realize that this light is full of intelligence and healing power ... this means ... that you are fully present in the now ... in a way that you can remember it at all times ... what you always have and had ... from now on you can deal with it and with this experience ... that you can now make ... and your experience about the presence of your higher self will develop further ...

... you will learn to listen to your inner guidance with more and more trust ... and with every relaxed breath you take ... more and more of the healing energy will open itself ... deeper ... and ... deeper ... more ... and more ... you are getting to know your true inner gentleness ... the best part of your soul ... beautiful ... and perfect ... since the beginning of you ... and even before that ...

... and please remember ... to keep in mind to always be connected with your inner gentleness ... and maybe you can imagine all your old, flwaed thoughts ... maybe as a symbol ...

(short break)

... and then you can simply dissolve these old and futile patterns of thought in the light ... that surrounds you ...

... enable yourself now ... to let every doubt ... and every hesitation ... simply dissolve in the light ... and you realize ... that these old feelings don't belong to you any longer ...

... Inhale this light, take in all the fresh oxygen, that reaches into every cell of your body through your unconscious mind ... relax with the feeling of this gentleness, that carefully touches every part of your being ... healing and bringing new energy where it is needed ...

... take part in the process by taking a deep breath ... and when you imagine the light, the healing and the loving energy, as they expand over your entire body ... with every breath you take ... deeper ... easily ... trouble-free ... with every breath ...

... no matter what feelings or thoughts come up ... they will dissolve, no matter if they are good or bad ... they glide into the healing light ... allow and invite all your thoughts and feelings to go into the light to be healed and to be changed to their well-being ... Imagine that you are standing straight and at ease next to your higher self, surrounded by loving energy ... realizing that this is the unconditional love of your own pureness ... the true integrity of your self, that is so pure, so free, that is not spoilt or reduced by anything ... it is not spoilt by anything that is thought or said ... or done ... not even by something that somebody else said about you ... or did to you ... or thought about you ... think about it now ...

... Your conscious mind in the energetic aura of higher self will re-evaluate your life experience ... your faith and your attitude ... in a certain manner ... you will be freed of what you need to be freed of, so that you can be in unison with the pureness of your original self ... in a way that flows unhindered

through you ... deeply breath this in ... again and again ... deeper and deeper ... your unconscious mind keeps all ... that is of value for you, of your life experience and the things you learnt ... everything that makes it easy ... to now go into completeness ... open your attitude for the presence and the energy of your higher self ... your true being ...

... Imagine a river with golden ... white light, that floats up till your head, from the source of endless love and healing intelligence ... imagine how it flows down to your heart ... and it fills your heart with love and healing energy ... it begins to beam trough your entire body ... it looks for a way through your being ... saturates every cell of your body with endless energy of love ... and you realize your true needs ... even if they are not yet known to you ... even if you were not aware of them until now ... on your way to completeness ...

Simply relax ... in this light ... and allow this river to fetch these needs ... to present them to the loving intelligence of the light .. as offerings and needs of pureness, healing and enlightenment ... invaluable knowledge of every kind ... for your well-being ... your will and the well-being of all beings ... simply be open ... make an inner gesture with your whole heart and soul ... so it may be ... relax in the light ... feel how it saturates and surrounds your body, in a protective and magnetic aura, that brings this blessing to you ...

You experience these wonderful, relaxing feelings ... think about thoughts, that flow into the light of your higher being ... ... you can now ask your higher self questions ... have an inner dialog in any way that you like ... I'm going to be silent for five minutes now or as long until you give me a sign by raising your index finger of your right hand ... if you understood me, raise the index finger of your right hand now. **Await the sign with the finger and give your partner five minutes time, or less if he or she raise his or her finger before this time ends.** *I am going to count from 1 to 5 and you will gain normal and awake consciousness, when I come to 5 ... and everything that you have learned and experienced today, will be beneficial for you and let you grow further ... you will develop further ... and develop a deeper connection between you and your true self ... and your normal, awake consciousness ... you are more awake and awake ... you are going to be able to express you own inner gentleness better and better ... joyful and in a manner that is best for you and the well-being of all beings ... now and for every moment to eternity ...*

6.4 The Quiet Voice Within

This | chapter will help you increase positive synchronicity[1]. The more a person is in union with his or her inner voice, the more positive choices he or she will make. Humanism[2] even assumes that a person always makes decisions for the greater good and well-being of the entire system.

Now ... in a few moments ... I want to help you increase your possibilities forever ... to show you from your inner-most being ... what is good and valuable within you ... and always has been ... long before you ever thought about it ... an inner system ... only for your well-being ... existing and maybe only laying there quietly ... anchored in your genes ... to safely accompany ... you and everything that will be ... through this wonderful world ...

... and now become aware ... of a quiet ... deeply lying ... inner voice within you ... maybe sleeping ... whispering ... this natural gift ... within you ... that knows what is good for you ... your wise and most faithful adviser ... independent ... and proof against bribes ... that, since your beginnings ... was always there ... and just is not listened to at some times ... through all the noise ... that comes in from the outside ... from people who think they have to think for you ... that pressure their beliefs or their views on you ... this wise ... inner advisor ... deep within you ... who has always been there ... and maybe just a little numbed ... because we humans often think other people know what is best for us ... how we should be ... or what we should do ...

Just approach this inner voice ... listen to its natural sound ... its source ... not the voice of other people ... that make you believe they know better ...

I am not interested in dictating something to you ... or to lead you in a certain direction ... or to reveal a belief or philosophy to you ... I am interested in increasing your skills ... in a healthy and positive way ... for your well-being ... because you already are full ... of what others think ...

Allow yourself to listen to you ... even if some outside noise may still irritate you ... you can still listen ... and welcome that quiet, inner voice ... listen to it more often from now on ... because you know all ... what it says to you ... already ... have always known ... it is your faithful ... loyal advisor ... companion ... fellow .. who always makes decisions with you ... even if you sometimes

---

1   sequence of events is called »synchronicity«, when the events cannot be put together in a direct correlation, but when it feels as if they belong together.

2   Humanism is a world-view and philosophy with origins in the occidental, ancient world. It focusses on interests, values and dignity of the single individual.

listen to it ... it instantly adapts ... to the new situation ... always allows you ... to think freely ... to decide on your own ... because your inner voice is proof against all bribes ... it is directly connected to your inner being ...

Even if it sometimes seems as if it has become lost ... that is because the noise from the outside has gotten louder ... and you have the chance to discover it anew ... for yourself and your well-being ... for the well-being of all living beings ... because your inner voice is not only incredibly loyal ... it also thinks coherently ... and was given to you, long before you were there ... before the birth of your parents ... or grandparents ... every human has it ... every human has the chance to discover it ... to rediscover it ... just like you are discovering it now ... and always ... if you listen to it ... you are going to realize that you are in unison with it ... with your inner self ... with yourself ... you are going to feel awake and present ... if you let it take part in your decisions ... you are going to realize how things will change for you for the good ... go well ... perfectly ... in the game of life ... where from now on you can play the games ... that will attain your goals ...

6.5 Hypnosis to Improve Learning

Many people have learning difficulties. Learning experience and uncoupling stress is tremendously helpful and beneficial. This is the main goal of the script.

Allow yourself ... to simply follow the sound of my voice ... just like before ... and we will start a series of sequences ... that can be very positive for you ... very beneficial ... when it comes to gaining new knowledge ... for your well-being ... and all that what lies deep within you ...

While you simply listen to my voice and relax ... let yourself go and for the next moments ... simply are able to relax ... without actively doing something ... even if life continues outside ... like always ... ever since ... long before our time ... you can ... because you have the skills for that ... simply absorb ... for a moment ... what you now notice ... all by yourself ... with no effort needed ... your unconsciousness will automatically look for the information needed ...

You would like to change something ... you want to change something ... but this is only a small part of the program ... because starting today an "I can" will be your constant companion ... while awake ... during hypnosis ... and in your dreams ...

And you will feel endless pride ... how productive you can be ... it is about attitude ... an inner approach ... to try more things ... rather than thinking about them ... to expand your reality ... to completely celebrate it ... with dignity ... and with pride ...

You now begin to accept your past and your past is an important piece ... of your development. A very important experience ... that you created ... when you now relax and let go ... for a moment ... avoid developing any form of guilt.

It is not of relevance for you ... at least it is not at all beneficial ... unnecessary for your experiencing from now on ... What you did in your past, was the best thing you could do at that time ... the best efforts you could make ... you learned from it, because now you see the past with the eye of the present time ... and when you are free from now on ... you can more easily do good for the people you love ... you evolved further and have grown ... you now understand that letting go of guilt is possible ... Only experience and education are of importance for you ...

Your childhood and your experiences were lead by the circumstances back then. You will keep things that you like and that suit you ... but all feelings, fears and doubts that live inside you, are no longer yours ... These things are accidents, you don't need to keep them. You can tick them off your list, as done and completed.

Begin to live every day according to your liking. You will grow quickly with this attitude ... new experiences will help you ... becoming the person you want to be ... you are going to be convinced that you are all you need to be successful, that you can have all the things you need for your success ... you feel that now and will always, every day anew ...

Now relax and experience this attitude. The only thing that you can do now ... is leaving the world out, go inside you, relax, and be aware of the fact that you can feel better in this moment than ever before ... This is reality. Use it.

... and begin to believe that all your positive and successful experiences of the past contain emotional, positive values for you. These feelings and emotions belong to you. Just like an old family member or a personal photo, they bring back positive emotions, buried emotions. They bring feelings back that you forgot. They spontaneously come back due to an event in your daily routine ... Become aware of these images and feel the same pride and the same happiness, that you experienced months or years ago when the event took place.

These feelings belong to you. Believe the best memories when they come to you. Relax and let yourself go. Feel ... how your body relaxed more and more. Relax more and more while you listen to my voice and the world ... drifts apart further and further ... While you listen to me, such positive thoughts come to you ... They will retrieve the best of you ... automatically ... If you ever felt proud, self-confident, encouraged or successful and longed for ... being something special ... then you can now use these feelings and this attitude ... Let it lead the way, like an honest, active part of your life ... for your purpose ...

You can use your best ... your best feelings ... They are just too valuable. Let these feelings revive ...

I want to practice with you ... to see things the way ... as they are in reality ... you develop yourself and feel great pride doing so ... your ability to achieve knowledge increases with every day ... and not only that ... you also have the chance to manifest this knowledge ...

You begin to recognize the final decision ... namely that it is up to you how you feel in a situation ... also when learning ... nobody can do this for you.

Nobody means to harm you and it is up to you if you let ... somebody control your life in any way. It is your decision ... not other people's ...

Your personality is one-of-a-kind ... you are unique in this world. You recognize ... that many people do things in a similar way ... but nobody is exactly like you ... because you are an individual ... and within you, you have a deep wisdom ... even when you learn and absorb knowledge ... greatly ... in your being ... Enjoy this feeling. It is true ...

Mistakes don't exist. There is no such thing. The grade of your success can only be valued by yourself. Even the smallest success is a seed of your future. It will grow and bloom, if you pay enough attention to it ... fear is always fantasy.

You alone decide how the world appears in your reality. Relax now ... Remember "I would, if I could ... I would" is a dream and a very good dream. "If I could" is the search for a plan or a way to make it come true for itself. "I can" is the harmony of all feelings and thoughts that bring success to your life.

You life will become easier and easier ... your unconsciousness allows you to find easier ways now ... because it knows just fine ... what you need ... but now without detours ... in your life ... while living ... wherever you need this experience ... It is done.

6.6 The Protective Shield

Sometimes, it is important to protect oneself from the outside, to not lose oneself and forget the process of creating by reacting to the outside. This protective shield technique helps you and your partner with this.

Drift off to a relaxed state ... and allow yourself and your body to relax and to rest a bit ... and while you glide a bit deeper, all things, that might distract you, seem to disappear ... yes, they can even help you to reach an even more comfortable state of hypnosis.

I want you to concentrate on your breathing ... breath in pure relaxation ... and breath out all your tensions ... feel, how all tension leaves you ... while you breath out ... you feel ... how you can glide into even deeper and deeper relaxation while you breath in ... your breathing is completely even ... so easy and effortless and you relax more and more ... and your entire body relaxes and you drift off into this relaxation further and further ... with every breath you take ... you feel a warm feeling of relaxation ... glide through your body.

And you can feel ... that some body parts ... and regions are easier to relax than others ... you feel this feeling in those body parts ... the most relaxed parts of your body ...

And you feel how these relaxed regions spread out to the rest of your body ... and while this remarkable ... warm and wonderful feeling ... of relaxation spreads over the rest of your body ... ... this feeling gets stronger and the relaxation simply spreads ... and while it does so, you wish ... to relax more and more ...

Simply imagine how this relaxation shines like light rays of sunlight in you ... comfortably warm and relaxing ... like ripples of water when a stone is thrown into a pond ... and the relaxation spreads over your entire body ... in every cell ... in every fiber ... in every bone ... and you enjoy this calm and peaceful relaxation in every part of your body ... and with every passing moment, this feeling of deepness, calmness, comfort and relaxation becomes stronger and every cell, every nerve and part of your body knows and enjoys this experience ... and this wonderful feeling now spreads out beyond the physical boarders of your body ... it spreads over yourself and surrounds you like a shield of protection ... and you can extend this feeling, as far as you want it to ... far ... beyond your body ... or really close to it, like a second skin ...

And since you created this protective bubble, this protective shield, you can do with it whatever you want ... you can use this shield however you want to ... the range of possible uses is endless ... it can be used as a filter for feelings or other things happening around you ... or to keep away unpleasant situations ... or, in a controlled way, let them in to gain experience ... or it can be used as a magnifier to make other people understand you better or for you to understand them better ...

And this protective shield can be visible or invisible for other people if you want it to be ... you can use this shield in every possible way ... and it is all right ... because this shield is your very own creation ... and you use it ... and enjoy all the comforts in every part of your body ... you can experiment with it ... you can expand this shield however much you want to ... and go to other places or other times with it ... and the more you use it, the stronger it will become ...

Notice how you feel at the moment ... you can now use this shield to get to your place of calmness and peace and deep, inner relaxation at any given time ... you use this shield and you feel how relaxation spreads over your entire body ...

6.7 The Inner Observer

This chapter helps your partner to gain new perspectives of his experiences. It is definitely exciting to ask these hypnotic questions and to look at things from a different angle. It is possible that your partner may be slightly confused afterwards. This is not entirely bad, being confused is a welcome state of learning new things.

If you simply ask yourself "Who are you?" ... then something really easy happens: you draw a line, a limit ... you begin to describe yourself ... while everything else out of this line is your "Not-You" ... your self, your identity ... as you know it ... is a line, a border from the inside out ... you are a human ... not a bird ... your self knows this ... you unconsciously draw a line ... between yourself and your environment ... "Who are you?" is a demand to draw a line ... Every answer, no matter on which level you may answer it ... scientifically, theologically ... or economically ... depends on ... drawing a line ... a line between you and your environment ... the exciting part of this line ... this border line ... is that it is movable ... It may be fascinating ... or even terrifying ... but I will now tell you what line we consider valid ... we all ... even you and me ... it is the line, the border known as skin ... everything within this skin border is you ... is me ... while everything outside of it is "Not-You" ...

Outside of this skin border, there is a "my" ... "my car" ... "my job" ... "my picture" ... "my TV" ... But there are also other borders ... additional borders within the skin border ... allow yourself to go a but further into your self ... **10 second break** *I invite you to explore your consciousness ... I invite you to move beyond your horizon ... that you might know, that others define for you ... allow yourself, for one moment, to be more than what you know of yourself ... what you call you "self" ... allow yourself to begin a wonderful journey full of experiences ... nothing of it will be true, if you don't want it to be ... nothing of what I tell you now, will carry you on or hold you back ...*
About one or two minutes break between the questions.

Give the partici-
pant two minutes
break, or more for
every question!

Simply answer those questions for yourself:

- *"Do youhave the feeling you have a body? Or do you feel like being a body?"*

- *"If you feel to have a body ... it is lying outside of your self ... because we realize that 'having' is outside of being ..." Answer the following question for yourself: "Do you feel like having feelings or do you feel like being feelings? Even if you feel like having feelings—which by itself is a weird way of putting it ... 'having', again, is outside of being ..."*

- *"Do you think you have feelings, or you are feelings?"*

- *"'Having' is outside of being ... Do you have thoughts ... ...or are you thoughts?"*

- *"'Having' is outside of being ... Do you have faith or are you faith?"*

- *"'Having' is outside of being ... Are you values or do you have values?"*

- *"'Having' is outside of being ... Are you the observer or do you feel like having an observer?"*

Now allow yourself to take in the answers, that you have just found. Take your own time. I will give you another two minutes, or maybe even a bit more, to take the things that are important to you back into your everyday consciousness. Two minutes break, or more.

6.8 Self-confidence

A high level of self-confidence helps in every situation. This chapter is for rediscovering your confidence.

Now, that you are completely relaxed, you feel free of all responsibility ... of all restraints ... of all opinion ... and of all fear ... you will now, very soon, in a few moments time, experience how it is when you are more self-confident ...

You already took an enormously big step by being willing to participate in hypnosis.

Begin to feel the power that motivates you to live a life full of joy and happiness ... your right given by nature ... from the beginning of time ... because it is in our nature ... to be happy ... begin to feel the strength that will blow away every doubt in you ... you will realize that everything bad will move away from you ... when you say "Yes" to yourself and your being and what remains, is self-confidence, strength and self-control ...

Self-confidence means ... to be aware of yourself ... to know that one is, to know what one is ... take a few moments time ... and concentrate entirely on your being.

30 seconds break

Love and happiness are basic laws of every human being, self-acceptance is a basic law. Observe yourself for a moment, all by yourself.

30 seconds break

This person deserves to be happy. The person, that you are observing ... so, you ... deserves to experience the natural state of love ... because the basis of loving others ... depends on ... being able to love oneself ... and you don't like or love people because of their success, you like or love others because of their being. And in the same way, it is possible ... to love the person you are observing right now ... Starting today, you will have the gift to be able to stand for this person ... Today is the first day of the rest of your life ... Take the chance ... the chance to enjoy a self-confident, free life.

Be aware ... that the first reason for a self-confident self is to feel well mentally. To feel well emotionally ... to feel well physically ... Simply be aware ... that you have the liberty and authority to fulfil your basic needs ... Realize now, that you are responsible for your life, no matter if you are currently suffering or enjoying it ... feel good or bad ... you are responsible for all consequences of your thoughts and acts ... Because of this it is important to have a good initial position and feel well mentally, physically and emotionally ... With positive feelings become aware of being the director of your life. Use the chances that arise and grasp them ... Begin to realize and accept your inheritance of wishing ... The mercy of wanting ... of demanding ... of daring ...

For the well-being of yourself and the others in your life, dare to ... because ... no mistake ... no punishment ... will ever be so severe ... that life in all its richness won't make it up for it.

6.9 The Temple of Healing

This chapter helps to activate the inner self-healing powers. Sometimes, it does not take much, to cause a lot ...

At the count of 3, you think yourself back into the time of the most famous Temple of Healing ever known ... 1 ... 2 ... 3 ... You now stand in front of the most famous Temple of Healing. (1 minute break) *Enter the temple, and please meet the physicians and priests, who are going to work with you ... Allow yourself to consider and find the best healers for yourself ...* (1 minute break) *And now, that you have found the best healers ... take a moment to talk with them ... they are going to tell you a number of valuable things ... that you can use ... to achieve real success ... for yourself ... your health ... and your well-being. Now, let yourself diagnose and test in all possible ways ...* (5 minutes break) *The diagnoses are made, and you now see yourself in the best of health and completely healed, with the physicians and priests, that participate in the healing process. See yourself in the best of health, leaving the old Temple of Healing, thinking yourself back into the present time, into which all feelings and energies, that you have developed and taken with you, can be brought with ... Then take a deep breath ... and strengthen the experience a bit ... before, in a moment, you open your eyes ... and in the meantime, feel this healing energy floating trough your body ...*

7 Ending

Ending a hypnosis is very simple. But in the setting of hypnosis still needs to be wrapped into a ritual. The participant can be given a waking signal or he or she can be given the permission to open the eyes, if he or she wants to.

No person can be hypnotized forever or is unable to end hypnosis on his or her own. This is a rumour, spread by uninformed people, that want to scare others, or who simply don't know any better.

Important to know

A constant ritual that is read to the participant to get his or her bodily functions get going again has the advantage of making him or her fit for a normal day in an instant.

My recommendation is to take back all suggestions that were only used to enforce the trance in a closure. For example the weight, lightness, warmth or alike.

7.1 Normal ending

This text is all you need to end the hypnosis. You can't do anything wrong. If you want to have your partner stay in trance and go into a sleeping state, use the text after the following one.

1. *Slowly, calmly and completely relaxed and light, you return to your full consciousness.*

2. *Every muscle in your body feels relaxed and easy, and you feel great.*

3. *Every cell of your body continues working perfectly fine ... you feel physically, mentally and emotionally strong and balanced ...*

4. *Maybe even allow your fingers to already move again slowly with the next number, feeling completely rested you will, open your eyes, take a good and deep breath and smile ...*

5. *Now simply open your eyes. Realize how you NOW are fully conscious, take a good, deep breath, stretch a little if you want to and allow yourself to smile.*

If your partner does not come out of the hypnosis, I would recommend reading the text again. If that does not help then wash his/her face with cold water and provide fresh air.

7.2 Transition to sleep

If you want to, you can now allow your mind to be calm and to enjoy the welcome relaxation and glide on into a wonderful and relaxing sleep. Thank you for letting me accompany you. The positive things that you encountered in your trance, will also accompany you in your dreams and strengthen the best in you even further.

8 A Few Insights in a Hypnotherapist's Life

These texts and tutorials have given you a few insights to what hypnosis can accomplish. But what distinguishes these texts from professionally performed hypnosis? This is exactly, what I want to show you with the following overview.

A professional hypnotist makes it his or her business to create the state of consciousness of hypnosis that can be used by the participant.

There are several possibilities to do so:

1. psychotherapy
2. medicine
3. coaching/counselling
4. hypnosis show

For medical purposes, hypnosis is used to reduce pain. For example in dentistry or in medical treatment where normal analgesics do not help any more, such as cancer treatment and palliative care.

In psychotherapy, hypnosis is used to treat mental disorders like fear, compulsion, psychosomatic conditions or sexual disorders. If you want to learn more about the work field of psychotherapy, I recommend my websites. There you can learn about the current state of research, the bandwidth of therapeutic possibilities and apprenticeship. You can find my website at the end of this book.

In most countries, a certification is needed for both medical and psychotherapeutic hypnosis and only physicians and alternative practitioner can obtain this certification.

In coaching and counselling, hypnosis is used to transform everyday processes. This means: learning to better do things one already knew or easier learning of new things. It is also allows one to observe things with more distance.

In hypnosis shows, hypnotic states are used with the permission of the hypnotized people to amuse an audience. Some of those experiments shown on stage are dangerous, like the cataleptic bridge[1]. Hypnosis shows often give a wrong impression of hypnosis, for example that the hypnotized person is completely at the hypnotist's mercy. Professional hypnotists see this as the most common reason for people having prejudices against the use of hypnosis.

8.1 Hypnotic Phenomena

There are many rumours about what possibilities a hypnotist has, that he can use for his or others' purposes. I summarized the most important hypnotic phenomena, that can be transformed by a professional using hypnosis:

- Association/Dissociation
- Prehypnotic Suggestion/Posthypnotic Suggestion
- Regression/Progression
- Hypersensitivity/Insensitivity
- Hypermnesia/Hypomnesia
- Slowing-down Time/Cutting down Time
- Flexibility/Catalepsy
- Positive Hallucinations/Negative Hallucinations
- Reliving/Repression
- Trance/Wakefulness

8.1.1 Association

Association means the connection of an outside stimulus with an emotion or a thought.

But also the emotions arising when listening to a song, or tightening muscles when seeing someone who causes us to feel unpleasant are a proof for

---

1 Cataleptic Bridge, in our context, means the state of making a hypnotised subject's arm, leg or back rigid.

association. It is the hypnotic term that is the closest to the psychological term of classical conditioning.[2]

8.1.2 Dissociation

Dissociation[3] is the ability of distancing one's feelings from a certain thing or topic.

A smoker, for example, isn't able to any more perceive the intoxication of his body caused by a cigarette as such. He or she feels the fighting for survival as relaxation. Dissociation means the splitting of the own body or of the consciousness. Dentists sometimes use dissociation to treat their patients without anesthetic.

8.1.3 Prehypnotic Suggestion

People with certain unhealthy attitudes are the best example for prehypnotic suggestions:

- "Women can't accomplish that."
- "You can't teach an old dog new tricks."
- "You will never understand anything when it comes to mathematics."
- "Too much fantasy is bad for your health."

and all the other phrases and sayings, that people hear from parents, relatives, teachers and others and one day have taken in although the sayings are dangerous for him/her. Of course there are also positive attitudes, patterns of faith and sayings belonging to prehypnotic suggestions. Every time a person begins a sentence with—"I am", he gives away something about his or her unique belief system and his/her relation towards his/her surroundings.

---

2   A term from Behaviourism that states how people can be intentionally trained for something, but that also makes them react in this certain, trained way by coincidental events due to assimilation to this training.

3   from the Latin »dissociare« - to estrange, to split

8.1.4 Posthypnotic Suggestion

Every suggestion made during hypnosis that has an effect, is a posthypnotic suggestion.

Examples:

1. The suggestion that the hypnotizes subject feels especially well after hypnosis.

2. The suggestion that the hypnotizes subject feels especially thirsty after hypnosis.

3. The suggesting of being free of pain during a dentist's visit.

Suggesting that enables the patient to feel self-confident and self-reliant, whenever he or she crosses the fingers (with the technique of anchoring[4]), is also considered a posthypnotic suggestion, coupled with the phenomenon of association.

8.1.5 Regression

The act of focussing on the past is called regression.

An old man who constantly thinks about World War II and has a panic attack every time there is thunder, because he thinks bombers are approaching, is showing signs of regression. He might also stash canned food "in case the Russians invade again".

8.1.6 Progression

Progression is the ability to set one's thoughts into the future and plan there.

Building a house, an employee planning his career with dreams and confidence or an athlete dreaming of the winning at the Olympics are all healthy examples of progression.

---

4   The technique of anchoring is a technique of neurolinguistic programming. It involves the saving of a certain emotion into a gesture, an act or into a symbol. During trance, the patient is given the imagination of feeling good. Now this good feeling is anchored to a pressure point on the body (for example: the therapist lays his hand on the patient's shoulder or the patient is asked to cross two fingers). After the trance's closure, the patient will experience this good feeling every time, when he or she feels this pressure point.

8.1.7 Hypersensitivity

People feel differently in different forms of consciousness. Sleepy or sleep-deprived, we tend to be far more sensitive then well-rested. Pain in general is a very subjective experience. Hypnotherapists try to alter these sensitivities in pain-therapy or at the dentists'.

8.1.8 Insensitivity

When some illnesses are very painful and uncomfortable, hypnotherapists use the state of hypnosis during operations and medical interventions at the dentist's or even in cancer therapy.

8.1.9 Hypermnesia

Hypermnesia is the ability to remember both good and bad experiences very well.

8.1.10 Hypomnesia

Hypomnesia is the opposite of hypermnesia. It is a certain forgetfulness that can occur in both old and young..

8.1.11 Slowing-down Time

People experience time differently, this is completely normal. People suffering from depression often complain about time passing too slowly. The boring French lessons in eleventh grade are a good example how I illustrate the slowing-down of time quite well.

8.1.12 Shortening Time

The shortening of time is the state experienced, when one does something fun and enjoyable. But there are people, who are constantly under stress and have the feeling that time is running away. This, too, is a subjective shortening of time.

8.1.13 Flexibility

People who have too little muscle tone, also suffer from a lack of flexibility, just like people who can't decide which way to go in life.

A student who can't decide which job to choose and in the end does not apply for any job, then tries this, then that, constantly changes his opinion, shows signs of flexibility.

8.1.14 Catalepsy

Catalepsy means rigidity. The hypnotherapeutic point of view suspects this as a reason for headaches and sacroiliac pain.

8.1.15 Positive Hallucinations

Phantom pain is a good example for positive hallucinations. The patient is feeling pain in a body part no longer existing. Alcoholics seeing white mice are also a common example.

8.1.16 Negative Hallucinations

People who constantly hurt themselves show this phenomenon, or people who no longer react to certain environmental stimuli.

8.1.17 Reliving

Similar to regression, people fall back into old memories and relive them as real with this phenomenon. When a person, who witnessed a bank robbery, breaks into sweat and starts trembling the next time he or she enters the very same bank because the person's unconsciousness thinks the situation is about to repeat itself, is showing signs of this phenomenon.

8.1.18 Repression

People who repress something try to not remember uncomfortable things. A woman who has been raped, but doesn't file charges and doesn't get psychological help, because she thinks "it is not that bad", might show signs of this phenomenon.

Repression can be a very useful defence mechanism, because it protects people from constantly dealing with unpleasant events. But regression might also cause grave somatic and psychosomatic illnesses.

8.1.19 Trance

Trance is the state a patient is in while under hypnosis. But there are people who are under hypnosis all the time. The boy known as daydreamer is a good example, because he doesn't concentrate on his every day life at school, but on his imagination and fantasy. But there are also people suffering from depression, who experience the world from another state of consciousness[5].

Some hypnotherapists assume that children up to an age of five years are in a constant state of trance; the partisan of transpersonal hypnosis (to which I as the author of this book belong) hold the view that people are always in a changed state of consciousness.

8.1.20 Wakefulness

People who are afraid of giving up control, who are under permanent stress or people with sleeping disorders all show signs of this phenomenon.

These people often are not easy to hypnotize. The therapist should give the patient the feeling that the patient is still in control of the situation.

---

5   Problemtrance, Erikson, Rossi 1972

9 Next steps

9.1 How Can I Learn All This?

Reputable hypnotherapists use this knowledge to help people to enjoy a self-dependent and free life. If you want to know more about hypnosis, I invite you to check out my website. There you can find a steadily growing pool of knowledge and information on the modern use of hypnosis in different areas of life. You can find my websites on the following page.

www.tnlp.de (Institute for transpersonal hypnosis and transpersonal NLP) My website is fast growing and will be updated and translated in english soon.

In America I recommend the course from Jack Elias to learn hypnosis fast and safe:

www.findingtruemagic.com

Jack is a great teacher. Please check out his channel on youtube.com, you will see with how much love he donate his teachings to us.

9.2 The Hypnotic Lessons of this Book as MP3s

Of course this book is meant to be an experience that you can share with another person. Naturally, there is also the possibility of experiencing it alone.

Feel free to check www.hypnoseverlag.de where you can buy the nine hypnotic lessons of this book as guided manual for 19,90 €. You also can find a constantly growing number of autogenous[1] hypnosis lessons that you can listen to for relaxation, healing and activating resources.

---

1 The term "autogenious" means "from within", meaning working on or by its own

10 About the Author

My name is Davor Antunovic and I work as a therapist, coach and instructor for hypnotherapy in my own practice in Esslingen am Neckar, a small city close to Stuttgart (famous for its automobiles like Porsche and Mercedes) Germany.

Since I first encountered hypnosis at the age of 14, the phenomenon fascinated my deeply. When I was 21, I finally had the chance to participate in my first hypnosis course. Ever since then, clinical hypnotherapy is my most effective tool in assisting other people to live a better life and improve their health.

For more than 10 years now I have studied the human consciousness with hypnosis, yoga, meditation, tantra, NLP and transpersonal psychology.

In my own practice in Germany, these concepts find their use in the real life of people like you and me. I made it my own business to learn with my clients, because nobody knows more about their personal problems than themselves.

A new era needs new ways of approaching our complicated mind. In our need to systematize, we follow a scientific tradition, that here, in the western society, is only just about 300 years old. Even worse: for the most parts, we have adopted half truths from our predeccessors and from oriental theories. If these concepts really worked, our economy would be functional, our policy would be authentic, our arms industry would be bankrupt and our hospitals only half as full as they are.

In this and in following publications, I invite you to the adventure of consciousness. Maybe, one day, we get to know each other personally and I come to know the story, how you discovered your consciousness.

German Websites:

- www.hypnoenergetics.de (webseite of my practice)

- www.tnlp.de (institution for apprenticeship in hypnosis and NLP)

- www.davorantunovic.de (seminars on Reality Creation)

- antunovic-laboratorium.de (webblog)

Further publications:

- Lehrbuch Hypnosetherapie/Handbook Hypnotherapy (coming soon in english!)

- Money Coaching – Mit Reality Creation zum äußeren und inneren Reichtum

- Money Coaching –Reality Creation Wealth Training (coming soon in english!)

11 Hypnosis in the United States

Jack Elias, CHT
Author of Finding True Magic
A certified NLP practitioner since l983, Jack Elias is recognized by the National Guild of Hypnotists and the Transpersonal Hypnotherapy Institute as a Clinical Hypnotherapist, and has trained in altered states processes and Ericksonian hypnosis. In addition, beginning in 1967 with five years of intensive Zen Buddhist practice, Jack continues over 40 years of practice and study of Buddhist and Siddha Yoga meditation and philosophy with recognized masters of these traditions.

Jack's book Finding True Magic is an acknowledged classic in the field. In a truly ground-breaking way, he blends the insights and disciplines of hypnosis, NLP and a variety of meditative techniques to create a dynamic process of change for his clients and students. Ormand McGill (deceased), the renowned "Dean of American Hypnotists" in the 20th century, said of Finding True Magic: "East meets West in TRUE MAGIC. Finding True Magic is a remarkable textbook on Transpersonal Hypnotherapy. Recommended for deep study."

Jack Elias is founder and director of the Institute for Therapeutic Learning, a Washington State licensed vocational school offering Transpersonal Hypnotherapy/NLP Certification trainings, seminars and mentorship programs in Seattle, Washington. Jack also offers private sessions for individuals, couples and families.

Jack's clients and students, including seasoned mental health professionals, psychologists, psychiatrists and other medical doctors—report that working with his transpersonal methods of hypnosis and hypnotherapy/NLP has helped them relate more effectively and meaningfully to their own clients and patients as well as to their families and themselves. It is Jack's mission to help people discover the powerful ability to get everything they really want. By accessing the true magic that exists in the mind, Jack says, we can meet any situation with confidence.

In his lively presentations to the business and professional communities internationally, Jack also draws on experiences in sales, management, and as an entrepreneur in applying these therapeutic techniques in professional contexts. Jack is also recognized as a skilled parenting counselor. He is a contributing author to the wonderful parenting book, If I Were Your Daddy, This Is What You'd Learn . This book is full of healing wisdom for every type of interpersonal relationship, even though it is a "Daddy" parenting book.

He is also a contributing author to the forthcoming book, A Fuller View, a collection of recollections and gratitude to Buckminster Fuller, for his guidance and inspiration by renowned people in a variety of fields of endeavor from science, to government, to human development.

Jack's Finding True Magic blog is a rich resource of insights and techniques that helps readers all over the world to clarify their thoughts and actions so they may build lives of success and joy.

The Institute for Therapeutic Learning is also known as the American Institute for Transpersonal Hypnotherapy/NLP. For training, counseling and coaching information, write to us at:

P.O. Box 17229
Seattle, WA 98127
or visit us at http://FindingTrueMagic.com
Email: info@findingtruemagic.com
Phone: 206 783 1838

Index